The Impressionists

Rosie Dickins

Illustrated by Freya Blackwood

Art history consultant: Kathleen Adler
Reading consultant: Alison Kelly, Roehampton University

Self Portrait
(1886)
by Monet

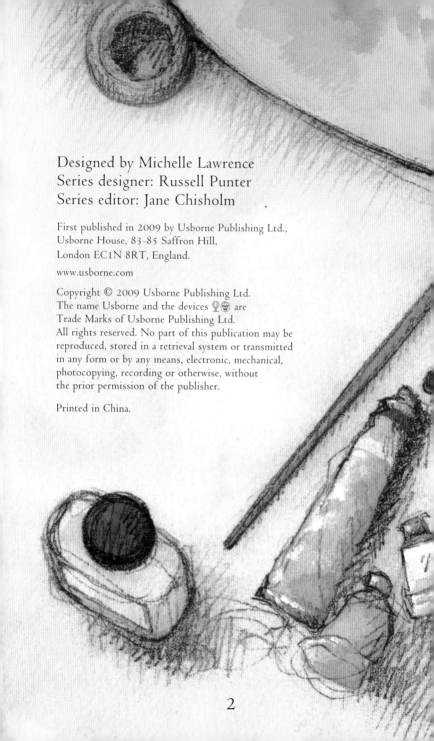

Designed by Michelle Lawrence
Series designer: Russell Punter
Series editor: Jane Chisholm

First published in 2009 by Usborne Publishing Ltd.,
Usborne House, 83-85 Saffron Hill,
London EC1N 8RT, England.

www.usborne.com

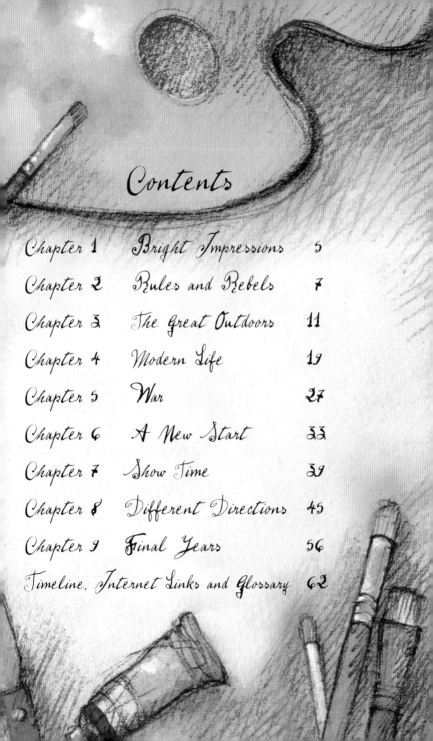

Contents

Chapter 1   Bright Impressions   5

Chapter 2   Rules and Rebels   7

Chapter 3   The Great Outdoors   11

Chapter 4   Modern Life   19

Chapter 5   War   27

Chapter 6   A New Start   33

Chapter 7   Show Time   39

Chapter 8   Different Directions   45

Chapter 9   Final Years   56

Timeline, Internet Links and Glossary   62

*Detail from **The Moulin de la Galette** (1876) by Renoir*

Pissarro

Cassatt

Degas

Morisot

Monet

Renoir

Sisley

Chapter 1
Bright Impressions

Sunlight sparkles on a tranquil lily pond; cobbled streets shimmer brightly after rain; women in ribboned gowns and men in top hats and cravats laugh and dance and play with their children...

Scenes like these, captured in loose strokes and swirls of paint, are the work of a group of artists known as the Impressionists – Claude Monet and Auguste Renoir, and their friends Camille Pissarro, Alfred Sisley, Berthe Morisot, Edgar Degas and Mary Cassatt.

Shimmering with light and colour, many Impressionist paintings are well-known and well-loved today. But it wasn't always so. Look at the picture by Renoir on the previous page – does it seem shockingly slapdash, garish and bright to you?

Yet when these pictures first appeared a hundred and fifty years ago, that was exactly how critics described them. The public was horrified. Hardly anyone would buy an Impressionist painting, and the artists who created them could often hardly afford a new tube of paint.

So who were these artists, and how did they come to be known as the Impressionists? The story begins in Paris, in the middle of the 19th century...

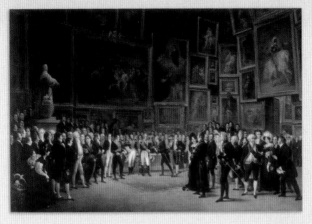

This painting shows a prize ceremony at one Paris Salon.

Chapter 2
Rules and Rebels
1862

In the 19th century, Paris was the capital of the art world. It was home to a famous art institute known as the Academy and, each spring, to the Salon – the world's biggest art exhibition.

To be successful, artists had to follow rules laid down by the Academy. These encouraged serious pictures of serious subjects – such as scenes from history or ancient myths – in dark colours and with a smooth, polished finish. But not all artists wanted to paint like that.

Two of the rebels were Claude Monet and Auguste Renoir. They had met while studying art at a small private studio in Paris and had quickly become friends. Now, to save money, they were sharing a room and living on boiled beans.

"What made you decide to become an artist?" Renoir asked his friend as they walked to class one morning.

Monet shrugged. "I could never stop drawing," he said. "First caricatures, then landscapes. I used to play truant from school to go sketching. A local artist told my family I should study art properly, and here I am!" He turned his dark, piercing gaze on Renoir. "What about you?"

Renoir ran a hand through his untidy reddish-brown hair. "I grew up drawing too – on the floor with my dad's bits of tailor's chalk. Then I got a job painting pictures on china cups, until they invented machines to do it instead. So really, there was nothing else left for me!" he laughed.

They ran up the steps to the classroom and began setting up their easels.

Each day, in a bare, brightly lit studio, twenty or so students gathered to practise figure drawing. While they sketched the hired model, the teacher – an established artist named Gleyre – wandered around and discussed their work with them.

Monet and Renoir were not star pupils. Their attempts were too rough and honest.

"Art isn't about drawing what you see," insisted Gleyre. "It's about beauty! Reality is full of flaws; the artist's job is to perfect it. Look at the old masterpieces in museums and you'll see. You should paint copies of all the great works."

"I'd rather paint the view from the window," muttered Monet.

At the end of the class, Gleyre looked at Renoir's brightly coloured figure and sighed. "You have skill, but you don't take things seriously enough!"

Renoir grinned mischievously.

The next day, he sketched the model using only Academy-approved browns and blacks.

"Look at the face I've given him," he whispered to Monet. "He looks like he's got stomach ache – Gleyre should love it!"

"Very good," nodded Gleyre, when he saw the finished piece. Monet and Renoir stifled their giggles, and his face fell. "Ah, when will you learn to take things seriously..."

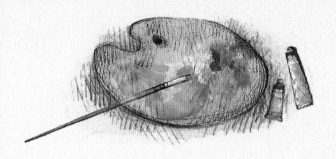

Chapter 3
The Great Outdoors
1863-65

Monet was finding Gleyre's lessons more and more frustrating.

"I want to paint light and truth and nature – not a model in a stuffy studio!" he said impatiently, one bright spring day.

A friendly student named Frédéric Bazille nodded. "It's true – the old art is finished. We ought to be out painting real life..."

"And real skies and real sunlight," interrupted a third voice. It was Alfred Sisley, a young English student.

Monet stood up. "Let's get out of here. We'll pack up our paints and take a train to the countryside."

So they clattered off to the station, laden with sketchbooks, canvases, folding easels, brushes, mixing palettes and dozens of tubes of paint. These tubes were still a recent invention and, because they were easy to carry and reseal, made it much easier to work out of doors. Earlier artists had had to prepare their paint laboriously from scratch, or store it in leaky leather pouches.

The steam train puffed rapidly out of Paris. Soon, they were passing open fields and scattered villages. Less than two hours later, they were at the edge of a forest of towering oaks and beech trees. They found lodgings at an inn and stayed for a week, exploring the forest and painting in the crisp, fresh air.

It was the first of many such trips. By the summer, an older artist named Camille Pissarro was joining them too. "The woods are my inspiration," he told them.

Spurred on by a sense of freedom and freshness, the friends were feeling cheerful about their work — and about their prospects at the Salon, too.

The Salon rules had just been changed,
in a way that seemed designed to encourage
newcomers.

"This is our chance," insisted Monet.

For artists, it was vital to get pictures
into the Salon. It meant official approval,
reviews in the papers, crowds of admirers
– and buyers.

The pictures in the Salon were chosen by a jury of Academy artists. In the weeks leading up to the show, the friends, along with hundreds of other hopefuls, sent in their best paintings.

They were to be bitterly disappointed. Out of all of them, only Renoir had a picture accepted. That year, the jury turned down nearly three thousand works – a record number.

"It's not fair," muttered Monet mutinously.

"The system is rotten," agreed Pissarro. "Everyone knows the juries just choose works by their friends."

Similar complaints could be heard all across Paris. Bowing to the protests, the authorities decided to show all the rejected pictures in a separate exhibition, so members of the public could judge them for themselves.

Dubbed the *Salon des Refusés* ("Salon of Rejects"), the alternative show was not a success. Most visitors left jeering or spluttering with indignation.

Lunch on the Grass *(1863) by Manet,*
often known by its French name, ***Le Déjeuner sur l'Herbe***

One painting, *Lunch on the Grass* by Edouard
Manet, caused a particular stir. It showed
a naked woman at a picnic. Nudity was all
very well in a historical setting, but this was
clearly set in the modern day, and the woman
was looking shamelessly at the viewer, instead
of turning modestly away.

Outraged, some viewers actually tried to
attack the picture and a guard had to be
posted in front of it.

Manet enjoyed the scandal. Like Monet and the others, he was no fan of the Academy. Unlike them, he came from a wealthy family and could afford to take risks.

When Monet and Renoir saw *Lunch on the Grass*, they admired its rebellious spirit.

"Things are changing, you'll see," Monet said, looking up at the huge canvas. "Future Salons will be different."

He was right. Over the next couple of years, the Salon juries, keen to avoid further scandal, did seem more open-minded. Renoir, Pissarro, Sisley and Monet all had pictures accepted.

Again, Manet caused a scandal, this time with a painting entitled *Olympia* – another naked woman in a modern setting, staring brazenly at the viewer.

To Manet's confusion, visitors were also telling him how much they liked his painting of the sea. "Sea painting? I haven't done any sea paintings!" he snapped. "Some young nobody must be taking advantage of my name!" He hunted down the canvas in question and peered at the signature. "That says *Mon*-et!"

Manet was cross, but he was also curious. A few months later, he tracked Monet down and introduced himself. Monet was very impressed by his confidence and cheerful disrespect for the Academy, and the two became friends.

Manet sympathised with Monet's dislike of classes. "*My* drawing classes bored me so much, I used to sketch the model upside down, just for fun," he said, with a grin.

Monet introduced Manet to Renoir and Sisley. In turn, Manet introduced two painter friends of his own: Edgar Degas and Berthe Morisot, both from wealthy Parisian families like his.

Degas dropped in to visit Monet in his studio. He stared intently at Monet's sea pictures, then scowled.

"What is it?" Monet asked nervously.

"The sun on the water is so bright, it hurts my eyes," replied Degas.

Monet laughed. "That's the best compliment anyone has ever paid me!"

But it was Morisot who turned out to share Monet's passion for painting outdoors. As a respectable young woman, she wasn't allowed to wander around the countryside alone, but she didn't let that stop her. Instead, she searched out picturesque spots in parks or places closer to home. Monet had found a kindred spirit.

Chapter 4
Modern Life
1866-69

Monet and the others began meeting more and more often – in their studios, at exhibitions, smart evening parties and long, smoky nights in local cafés. They eagerly discussed art and politics and the problems with the Salon.

One evening, the subject turned to colours, and the new chemical-based paints now available in the shops.

"They look much brighter than the old colours," said Monet happily. "Especially if you use a white undercoat. They're great for painting sunshine."

"But the brightest effects come from the contrasts between colours," Pissarro joined in. "Blue and orange, say, or red and green..."

"Been reading up on colour theory again, have you?" laughed Manet.

"But it's true. We need to find a new range of colours," said Renoir. "The Academy artists fill their pictures with gloomy blacks, but even shadows have colour. I realized that when I was painting in the forest."

"Of course you've got to get things down quickly, and keep your colours fresh," said Manet. "But why do it outside? You can paint better in the studio, without getting rained on or interrupted by every passer-by."

"In the studio?" moaned Monet. "How can you capture the exact effect of the light?"

"Well, of course you can make sketches outside..." began Manet.

"Sketches?" cried Monet. "I want to make finished pictures, not sketches!"

Degas frowned. "Personally, I always start by making sketches," he said. "For me, art is about imagination and hard work, not being on the spot." Monet snorted.

"Photography is going to change art,"
Degas went on. "Why try to imitate how
things look, when the camera can do that
for you?"

Here, a man with ink-stained fingers
interrupted. It was Charles Baudelaire, a
local poet. "Chemicals, cameras, all these
modern inventions," he said. "This is a
wonderful age. But you wouldn't know it
from all those old-fashioned scenes in the
Salon. Where are the city streets, the train
stations, the people in ordinary clothes?
What we need is a painter of modern life!"

Manet nodded. "A painter of modern life," he repeated. "That's it!" He turned to Monet – only to find his friend disappearing in the direction of a dark-eyed young woman walking past the café. It was Camille, Monet's new model.

Camille, in a detail from
Women in a Garden
(1866) by Monet

Renoir winked at Manet. "I think our friend is in love," he whispered.

Renoir was right. Monet and Camille were soon spending all the time they could together. But when Monet's relatives found out, there was a huge row and they cut off his allowance. It wasn't much, but he and Camille needed every penny, especially after their son, Jean, was born.

It was a difficult time for Monet. Torn between his relatives and his new family, and constantly worried about money, he became so depressed that he thought about ending his life. He threw himself into the river – but the cold water brought him to his senses. He clambered out, dripping, and set about changing his life.

With a bit of luck and some help from Bazille, he sold a few pictures and scraped together enough money to set up house properly with Camille. Slowly but surely, things began to improve.

Monet and Camille settled in the suburbs, not far from Renoir, and the friends began painting together again.

23

On warm summer days, they met by the river and walked along the bank to a floating cafe known as *La Grenouillère* ("The Frog Pond"). It was a beautiful place, surrounded by rustling trees and rippling water, and popular with daytrippers, who came to swim and mess about in boats.

Here, the friends set up their easels and worked side-by-side in the sunshine.

*Close-up of **La Grenouillère** (1869) by Renoir*

Monet captured shadows and reflections with broad stripes of blue, brown and white. Renoir painted people and trees with soft, feathery dabs of colour.

"That's pretty," said Monet, gazing at his friend's delicate brushwork.

Renoir smiled. "Art should be pretty," he answered. "There are enough unpleasant things in the world already."

But the jury at the next Salon didn't agree. Although Manet had a few pictures accepted, Monet, Renoir and the others were flatly turned down – and this time, there was no Salon des Refusés.

"If no one can see our work, no one will buy it," grumbled Monet. "We'll be ruined!"

"There's only one solution. Let's put on our own exhibition!" said Bazille boldly.

Manet shook his head. "How many people would come? The Salon is the only place worth showing."

Still, everyone else liked the idea. They talked about it at length and parted for the summer feeling newly hopeful.

Monet and Camille went to the seaside. Pissarro took his wife and children to the country. None of them had any idea of the dangerous times looming ahead...

*Detail of Camille from **The Beach at Trouville** (1870) by Monet. This was painted on the spot — if you look closely, there is sand stuck to the paint.*

Chapter 5
War
1870-71

In July 1870, after years of bickering, France declared war on neighbouring Prussia (now part of Germany). Suddenly, the friends had no time to discuss exhibitions – only how best to defend themselves and their country.

Men of fighting age began to enlist. Bazille joined the army, Degas signed up for the National Guard defence force and Renoir ended up in the cavalry.

"Even though I've never been on a horse before," he told the others, grinning.

Sisley fled to England, but Morisot stubbornly remained in Paris. Pissarro and Monet, with families to worry about, stayed in the countryside and prayed the fighting wouldn't reach them.

Pissarro had chosen the wrong place to wait. A few months later, news came – the Prussians were advancing.

"Quick, get the children," Pissarro told his wife. "We need to leave at once." There was no time to pack. Most of his paintings had to be left behind.

The fighting dragged on. During one skirmish, Bazille was killed, leaving his family and friends devastated.

After a bitter struggle, the French generals surrendered. But the war was not over. In Paris, furious crowds took to the streets, determined to stop the Prussians from entering their city.

Manet hid his paintings in a friend's cellar. "In case of looting," he explained.

Morisot's garden was full of camping soldiers. Men did military practice in the streets while smoke rose ominously in the distance. Wounded soldiers were brought back from the front line and the grand exhibition rooms of the Salon were turned into a makeshift hospital to house them.

Explosive shells began falling on the city. Then Prussian forces surrounded it. Under siege, life got harder. Food and fuel soon ran low. Shops and restaurants began selling meat from dogs, cats and rats. People shivered miserably as they picked their way through muddy streets in search of supplies. Weak from lack of food, many fell sick.

Meanwhile, down on the coast, boats had been busy ferrying refugees across the sea to England, including Monet and Pissarro and their families. The two friends spent the winter painting in London, fascinated by the effects of sunlight on snow and fog.

They also met a young French art dealer, a refugee from the war like them. His name was Durand-Ruel, and he began buying their work with enthusiasm.

Close-up of **Fox Hill, Upper Norwood** (1870) *by Pissarro — one of several paintings he made while in London, showing the area where he was staying.*

Back in France, the following year, the city finally surrendered. The siege was over, but life didn't get any easier. There were food riots and yet more fighting, this time by rebellious workers trying to oust the French government and set up an independent mini-state, known as the Paris Commune.

Renoir returned from his regiment to find the city was still a dangerous place. One bright, cold day, he was sketching by the river when a group of rebels spotted him.

"Look at those drawings," said one. "He's mapping out the area – he must be a government spy. Arrest him!"

They dragged Renoir to headquarters and threatened him with execution. Luckily, a journalist recognized him and persuaded the others to release him.

The rebels had reason to be suspicious. Government forces were poised to attack. The rebels were no match for trained troops. After a week of bloody fighting, it was all over, and thousands of men and women who had supported the Commune were sent to prison, deported or executed.

Morisot — who had left the city just before the final attack — returned to find it full of rubble and ruined buildings. "It's like a bad dream," she whispered.

The old friends were in a bad way. Renoir was sick and haunted by Bazille's death. Many banks and businesses had collapsed, leaving Sisley and Degas short of money. And Pissarro's house was a ruin. He returned to find it looted, with the roof smashed in and paintings ripped apart, the canvas used as rags and floor coverings. "All those years of work, gone forever," he sighed.

A Japanese print from Monet's collection

Chapter 5

A New Start

1872-73

After the war, life slowly returned to normal. Monet came back from his travels fired with a new passion – Japanese prints.

"Look at these," he told Degas, getting out his collection. They were elegant and stylish, and often caught scenes from unusual angles. Degas loved them.

The streets of Paris echoed with the sound of workmen rebuilding the city. Peace brought a buzz of prosperity. Renoir went out and painted the fashionably dressed crowds, getting his brother to delay passersby with pointless questions so he had more time to sketch them.

Sales began to pick up for the artists, too. New art galleries appeared, and Durand-Ruel opened a second shop. To fill it, he spent thousands of francs buying dozens of works by Degas and Manet.

Monet was also selling more pictures than before. With his money, he rented a house in the suburbs, where he painted happily – Camille and little Jean in the garden or strolling through the fields, and sunny views of the nearby river.

*Close-up of **Wild Poppies, Near Argenteuil** (1873) by Monet. Camille and Jean appear twice.*

Sisley and Manet sometimes came and painted with Monet. Manet laughed to find his friend working in a little boat. "Don't you mind all that bobbing around?"

"No," said Monet. "I get a better view of the water like this."

Pissarro also moved to the suburbs. Visitors found him in the middle of a chaotic household full of children and animals, or out painting the local landscape, with its farms, orchards and old stone cottages.

*Close-up of **The Cradle** (1872) by Morisot*

In Paris, Morisot was painting her sister and her sister's children. One famous image shows her sister beside a cradle, delicately capturing the anxiety of a new mother.

Morisot was feeling wistful about her own lack of family. "Painting is just heartache and trouble," she sighed.

But consolation was at hand, in the form of Manet's younger brother, Eugène. After a whirlwind courtship, the two married.

Also in Paris, Degas was busy with the city's nightlife – flickering, gaslit scenes of people in theatres, cafes and bars, often seen from unexpected angles. He also began a series of ballet dancer pictures, which would occupy him for the rest of his life.

The Dance Class (c.1873) by Degas

Once again, the friends began meeting to talk about art and their old idea of an independent exhibition.

"It'd be great publicity," said Monet.

"We could get everyone to come," added Pissarro. "Not just wealthy Salon types."

Manet frowned. "Count me out. It's career suicide! The Salon is the route to success."

But the others' minds were made up.

It only remained to work out how to organize things. They decided to form a "Company of Artists" which anyone, not just the friends themselves, could join. In exchange for a small subscription fee, members could exhibit whatever they liked.

"No juries," said Monet, smiling.

To house the show, they rented a big, glass-fronted studio overlooking a fashionable street. Degas signed up more members. Then they printed posters and catalogues. Eventually, they were ready.

Box at the Theatre (1874) *by Renoir*

Chapter 7
Show Time
1874

The group's first exhibition opened in April 1874, with 165 pictures by 33 artists. The paintings on show included Renoir's *Box at the Theatre*, Monet's *Impression: Sunrise*, Morisot's *Cradle* and Degas' *Dance Class*, as well as landscapes by Pissarro and Sisley – all now considered masterpieces.

Unlike the Salon, where pictures were crammed in any old how, the paintings were arranged by artist and hung neatly in rows. On the blood-red walls of the studio, they made a striking sight.

Entry cost just one franc. The exhibition ran for a month and attracted around a hundred visitors a day – but many of them walked out laughing, or angrily demanded a refund. Compared to the dark, polished pictures they were used to seeing at the Salon, such vivid colours and sketchy brush strokes seemed crazy or carelessly slapdash.

"Don't these people know how to draw?" fumed one elderly gentleman. "Or can't they be bothered to finish things properly?"

One picture especially stood out – Monet's *Impression: Sunrise*, a misty, indistinct view of a harbour at dawn, dashed onto the canvas in rapid, blurred streaks. The word "impression" seemed to describe the whole spirit of the exhibition, leading critics to nickname the group "Impressionists".

Impression: Sunrise, Le Havre (1872) *by Monet*

It was not meant to be a compliment.

"Hopeless, grotesque confusion," ranted one critic, "the negation of the most elementary rules of drawing and painting".

"Palette-scrapings on a dirty canvas," mocked another. "Wallpaper in its earliest state is more finished."

There were some more kindly reviews and a few sales. Sisley did best, earning a thousand francs, but the others hardly sold anything.

In the end, they didn't even cover their costs. When they added up the accounts, each exhibitor owed nearly 200 francs.

"There's nothing for it," sighed Degas. "We'll have to dissolve the company. All in favour?" The vote was unanimous.

Despite the problems, they didn't abandon the idea of exhibiting together. All in all, between 1874 and 1886, there would be eight shows. These are now known as the original Impressionist exhibitions. But the group taking part changed each time, as individuals fell out or tried sending their new pictures to the Salon instead. Only Pissarro joined in all eight shows.

There was no sudden breakthrough. Despite a handful of good reviews, the insults kept coming. Critics described the second exhibition as the work of "five or six lunatics". As for the third show, "children entertaining themselves with paper and paints do better".

Le Revue

Lunatic artists hold new exhibition

Pissarro's use of colour drew particular fury. "Trees are not violet; the sky is not butter," fumed one reviewer. "No sensible human being could tolerate such defects."

"At least we're getting attention," said Morisot bravely.

"That's all very well," sighed Pissarro. "But how will I feed my family?"

The harsh reviews left the artists dejected. Their frustration led to frequent squabbles, though Pissarro tried to keep the peace.

Someone jibed that Monet and Sisley kept churning out the same pictures. "We can't flood the place with endless river views!"

Monet, in turn, didn't want to admit too many new members. "We can't open our doors to the first dauber who comes along," he said grumpily.

But others were more open. Degas had become friends with a young American painter named Mary Cassatt and invited her to join the fourth show. She readily accepted. "At last, I can stop worrying about the jury," she told Degas happily.

Cassatt, like Morisot and Degas, had a wealthy family behind her. She didn't have to sell paintings for a living. But for the others, it was often difficult to find the money for paints, or even food.

Things were especially hard for Pissarro, with a growing family to support – all the more so when Durand-Ruel ran into trouble and stopped buying new works. Sometimes, in desperation, Pissarro gathered up an armful of pictures and trudged around Paris in search of buyers, walking to save on bus fares and counting every penny.

Raffle
1st Prize

Chapter 8
Different Directions
1875-81

As the poor exhibition reviews flooded in, the friends tried to think of other ways of selling pictures. "We could hold an auction," suggested Renoir. Monet, Sisley and Morisot agreed to try it, but this idea fared no better. The auctioneers couldn't tell which way up to hold the paintings, and the crowd jeered. The insults nearly led to a fist fight.

Pissarro tried a different tactic — a raffle, with one of his paintings as first prize. With the help of a friend who ran a restaurant, plenty of tickets were sold. But the winner, a young servant girl, was disappointed with her prize and quickly swapped it for a cream bun.

Still, the group had begun to find a few private buyers. A rich department store owner named Ernest Hoschedé bought a few of Monet's pictures, including *Impression, Sunrise*, and a wealthy publisher named Georges Charpentier bought some pictures from Renoir.

Charpentier also commissioned Renoir to paint his family in their fashionable luxury apartment.

"Aren't you envious when you visit them?" asked Monet wistfully.

"No," laughed Renoir. "Gold is all very well for picture frames, but I don't need gold taps in my bathroom!"

The finished portrait was good advertising. Such a rich, stylish home was just what many people aspired to. Soon, Renoir had a steady demand for similar pictures.

Renoir's personal project, however, was rather different. He had discovered an open-air dance hall, the *Moulin de la Galette*, where young workers went in their best clothes, to gossip and dance in the sunshine.

Fired with enthusiasm for the place, he decided to do something big. He spent the summer getting to know the regulars and making dozens of sketches. Then, he bought an enormous canvas and began to paint...

Dance at the Moulin de la Galette (1876) *by Renoir.*
In real life, the figures in the foreground are almost life-size.

The result was a dazzling sunlit scene. But when it was exhibited, it baffled viewers.

"I don't come to galleries to look at working class dance halls," shouted one gentleman angrily. "This isn't *art!*"

Renoir shrugged off the attack. He was enjoying his carefree life in Paris. "I've nothing in my pockets but my hands," he used to say. "But at least I've no family to worry about."

All that changed when he met a pretty, red-haired seamstress named Aline. Merry and down-to-earth, she charmed Renoir. First he asked her to model for him – and then he asked her to marry him.

Aline's mother was horrified. "A penniless artist!" she snorted.

But Aline said yes anyway. "I don't know anything about art," she told Renoir cheerfully, as he gazed intently at her, then brushed colours delicately onto his canvas. "But I love watching you paint."

Aline posed for some of Renoir's most famous paintings, including *The Lunch of the Boating Party*.

This was painted on the terrace of a riverside restaurant, not far from La Grenouillère. It was a favourite spot with Renoir, who often ate there, paying for his meals with pictures. On sunny weekends, the place filled with people going out on boats. Renoir took Aline there too. Together, they went boating and swimming, and danced on the terrace in the evenings.

The Lunch of the Boating Party (1881) by Renoir.
Aline is sitting on the left, holding a small dog.

Monet was less happy. He and Camille had been spending far too much and were running out of money. Monet wrote begging letters to his friends, and tried hard to make sales. "I'll paint trash, if it pays the rent," he sighed.

Hoschedé helped by buying a few works, and invited Monet to come and paint his country house. Monet stayed for months, and became friends with Hoschedé's whole family.

Degas had retreated to his studio, where he was painting "open-air" scenes by getting his model to sit on the floor. "A crumpled cloth is all I need to do a sky," he muttered.

He continued his scenes of nightlife in the studio too, hiring models and dancers to pose for hours, snapping crossly if they moved a muscle. Problems with family and finances were making him short-tempered.

Cassatt and Morisot were still living comfortably with their families. Cassatt was experimenting with print-making with Degas. Morisot, happily married, was busy painting household scenes. But she longed for a child.

So she was delighted when her daughter, Julie, was born. Julie instantly became her favourite model.

Sisley and Pissarro were living and working outside Paris, where the rents were cheaper. To help feed her family, Pissarro's wife grew vegetables, and kept rabbits and hens, but life was a constant battle – so she was dismayed when their oldest boy, Lucien, told her he was planning to become an artist like his father.

"How does anyone make money out of art?" she complained.

Saint Lazare Station (1877) *by Monet*

Meanwhile, Monet had been brooding over the critics. "Idiots," he told Renoir. "They want to see everything clearly, even fog! I'll show them what fog *really* looks like."

"You're mad," laughed Renoir.

But Monet had made up his mind. He went to Saint Lazare Station, where steam trains filled the space with billowing smoke.

"I've come to paint the city's *best* station," he told the station director grandly.

Flattered, the director halted trains and ordered the drivers to let off extra steam.

The result was half a dozen startlingly modern paintings, all of which Durand-Ruel immediately bought. Delighted, Monet went home and celebrated by buying flowers, fine foods and wines. But he didn't really have enough money to pay for it all and soon he was broke again.

Life got more complicated when Monet's buyer and friend, Hoschedé, was suddenly declared bankrupt and thrown out of his country house. Now it was Monet's turn to help. He offered to take in Hoschedé's wife, Alice, and her six children.

On a painting trip, Monet discovered a pretty riverside village with a house to rent. The house was big enough for both families. He took it straight away.

But the weather was bad and the house was cold – and it was becoming obvious that Camille was seriously ill, possibly with cancer. Monet sent for doctors, but they couldn't help. Alice and his friends did their best to keep him going, but Monet felt powerless.

"My life is a failure," he declared bitterly.

Camille finally died in 1879. Stricken with grief, Monet threw himself into his work. Alice looked after the house and children while he spent hours outside in the biting cold, painting a string of frozen winter scenes.

At last, slowly, the friends' luck began to change. Their fourth exhibition attracted nearly 16,000 visitors and even made a small profit. Encouraged, they planned a fifth and then a sixth show, although first Renoir and then Monet dropped out of the group.

Durand-Ruel was doing good business, too. He bought thousands of francs worth of pictures from Monet.

As for Sisley, "I'll take *everything* you paint," Durand-Ruel told the startled painter, "in exchange for a regular salary."

Determined to publicise the group, Durand-Ruel organized a seventh exhibition, with delicate portraits by Morisot, leafy landscapes by Pissarro and Sisley, breezy sea paintings by Monet and *The Lunch of the Boating Party* by Renoir.

"Soon, people will call these masterpieces," Durand-Ruel said confidently – and he was right. The exhibition was a great success. Wealthy art lovers queued to see it and the reviews were better, too.

"Monet is a poet of nature," one critic wrote admiringly.

Durand-Ruel also arranged an exhibition in New York. It sold so many pictures that he opened a permanent New York gallery. Thanks to his efforts, the Impressionists were at last beginning to enjoy some prosperity. It had been a long struggle.

Chapter 9
Final Years
1882 onwards

It was twenty years since the friends had first met — twenty years filled with different artistic ideas and directions. Now they were growing old and competing with younger artists

The passage of time took its toll. Camille's death was followed by the death of Cassatt's sister, which left Cassatt devastated and hardly able to paint — and more tragedy was to come.

Manet was seriously ill, though he ignored it and doggedly went on painting. To his delight, he won the prestigious Legion of Honour medal — but could scarcely walk to accept it, because of an infection in his foot. In the end, doctors decided to amputate. After the operation, he fell into a raging fever and died.

Manet had never really been part of the group, but he had always been an inspiration to it. The friends felt his death deeply.

Sisley went on living quietly in the country, gradually losing touch with the others. Despite Durand-Ruel's best efforts, Sisley had few buyers and became very disillusioned, but he kept painting until he died.

Pissarro struggled along with his family, as full of ideas and hope as ever. Recognition came at last when two of his pictures were bought by a famous museum. He would never be rich, but he had no regrets. "At least I've managed to live by my ideas," he said.

Close-up of **Banks of the River Loing** *(1885) by Sisley*

Degas was working alone in his little city studio. Sometimes, he regretted his lack of family. "All these dancers have sewn up my heart in pink satin," he sighed. As he grew older, his eyesight began to fail, but he stubbornly continued sculpting and sketching from memory.

Morisot began taking her daughter, Julie, with her on drawing trips. But on one trip, Julie caught 'flu. Morisot nursed her better, only to fall sick herself. She died soon after.

Cassatt was still successfully painting and making prints. But, like Degas, she was slowly losing her sight. Eventually, virtually blind, she had to stop.

Renoir went on painting while Aline raised their sons. As he grew older, he suffered from arthritis. Eventually, his fingers became too stiff to grasp a brush. But, with his family's help, he continued to paint using a brush strapped to his hands. "I think I'm beginning to understand something about it," he said, just before he died.

Monet moved to a tiny hamlet named Giverny, where he rented a house with pink walls and a garden by the river. Alice came with him, to run the house and look after the children — and when Hoschedé died a few years later, the two were married.

Now, Monet began work on series of pictures, painting the same scene — a golden heap of drying hay, a twisting line of trees or an ornate stone cathedral — again and again, in different lights. The series proved very popular and, by 1890, he had enough money to buy the house at Giverny.

He immediately set about creating a huge water garden, which still exists today. He dammed the river to create a vast pond, which he filled with every kind of water lily. Local farmers worried such exotic plants might poison the water, but he kept on.

A few years later, Monet began his most famous series — water lilies. These pictures capture a watery world of lilies and trees and reflected clouds, seen from dawn to dusk.

In old age, Monet suffered eye problems, but he kept on painting lilies, creating huge, tranquil expanses of colour. He died in December 1926, the last of the true Impressionists.

But although the Impressionists are no longer with us, their art lives on.

The Water Lily Pond (1899) by Monet – just
one of several hundred lily paintings he made.

Today, their paintings draw enormous
crowds to museums and art galleries, and
sell for tens of millions at auction. Copies
of their pictures are all around us, in books
and on posters and cards – a constant
reminder of the rebel artists whose vision
changed art forever.

Impressionism Timeline

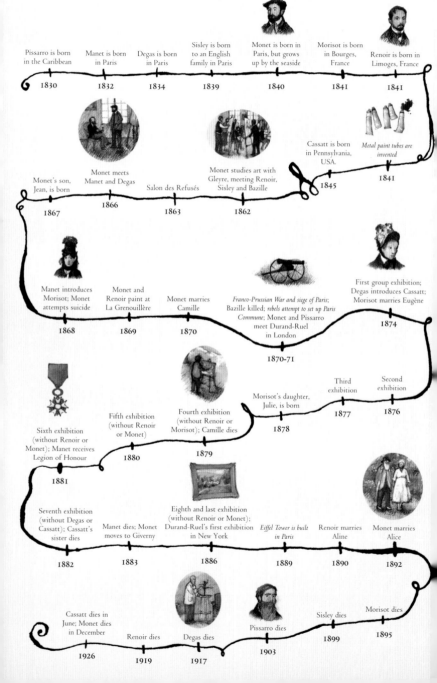

Pissarro is born in the Caribbean — **1830**

Manet is born in Paris — **1832**

Degas is born in Paris — **1834**

Sisley is born to an English family in Paris — **1839**

Monet is born in Paris, but grows up by the seaside — **1840**

Morisot is born in Bourges, France — **1841**

Renoir is born in Limoges, France — **1841**

Cassatt is born in Pennsylvania, USA. — **1845**

Metal paint tubes are invented — **1841**

Monet's son, Jean, is born — **1867**

Monet meets Manet and Degas — **1866**

Salon des Refusés — **1863**

Monet studies art with Gleyre, meeting Renoir, Sisley and Bazille — **1862**

Manet introduces Morisot; Monet attempts suicide — **1868**

Monet and Renoir paint at La Grenouillère — **1869**

Monet marries Camille — **1870**

Franco-Prussian War and siege of Paris; Bazille killed; rebels attempt to set up Paris Commune; Monet and Pissarro meet Durand-Ruel in London — **1870-71**

First group exhibition; Degas introduces Cassatt; Morisot marries Eugène — **1874**

Sixth exhibition (without Renoir or Monet); Manet receives Legion of Honour — **1881**

Fifth exhibition (without Renoir or Monet) — **1880**

Fourth exhibition (without Renoir or Morisot); Camille dies — **1879**

Morisot's daughter, Julie, is born — **1878**

Third exhibition — **1877**

Second exhibition — **1876**

Seventh exhibition (without Degas or Cassatt); Cassatt's sister dies — **1882**

Manet dies; Monet moves to Giverny — **1883**

Eighth and last exhibition (without Renoir or Monet); Durand-Ruel's first exhibition in New York — **1886**

Eiffel Tower is built in Paris — **1889**

Renoir marries Aline — **1890**

Monet marries Alice — **1892**

Cassatt dies in June; Monet dies in December — **1926**

Renoir dies — **1919**

Degas dies — **1917**

Pissarro dies — **1903**

Sisley dies — **1899**

Morisot dies — **1895**

Internet Links

You can see lots more Impressionist paintings, and find out more about the artists who created them, by going to the Usborne Quicklinks Website at **www.usborne-quicklinks.com** and typing in the keyword 'Impressionists'.
Please note that Usborne Publishing cannot be responsible for the content of any website other than its own.

Glossary of Art Words

Academy - official art institute, founded in 1648 in Paris, which organized the Salon
canvas - fabric surface used for painting
easel - wooden frame used to prop up a canvas while painting
Impressionism - a painting style known for its sketchy, broken brushwork and bright, unmixed colours; Impressionist pictures are usually made on the spot, in the open air, so as to capture an immediate impression, rather than an exact likeness
Impressionists - a loose grouping of artists who helped to develop Impressionism and who exhibited together between 1874 and 1886
Japanese prints - traditional Japanese pictures made by printing from carved wooden blocks
palette - board used for mixing paints; also the range of colours used by an artist
oils, or **oil paints** - paints made by blending pigments (coloured powders) with slow-drying oils
open-air painting - painting outside, in natural light; sometimes known by its French name, *plein air*
Salon - official art exhibition organized by the Academy and the French authorities
Salon des Refusés - exhibition of pictures refused entry into the official exhibition

Index

Academy, 7, 10, 14, 17, 20

Cassatt, 5, 43, 44, 50, 56, 58

critics, 6, 40, 41, 42, 55

Degas, 5, 18, 20, 27, 32, 33, 34, **37**, 38, 39, 42, 43, 44, 50, 58

Durand-Ruel, 30, 34, 44, 53, 55, 57

exhibitions, 7, 14, 19, 25, 27, 38, 39, 40, 42, 45, 54, 55

Giverny, 59, 60

light, 6, 11, 20, 60

London, 30

Manet, 5, **15**, 16, 17, 18, 20, 22, 23, 25, 28, 34, 35, 36, 38, 56, 57

Monet, **1**, 5, 8, 10, 11, 13, 14, 16, 17, 18, 19, 20, **22**, 23, 25, **26**, 27, 30, 33, **34**, 35, 38, 39, 40, **41**, 43, 45, 46, 50, **52**, 53, 54, 55, 59, 60, **61**

Morisot, 5, 18, 27, 28, 32, **36**, 39, 43, 44, 45, 50, 55, 58

New York, 55

paints, 12, 19, 42, 44

Paris, 6, 7, 8, 12, 28, 31, 33, 44, 48, 50

Pissarro, 5, 12, 14, 16, 20, 26, 27, 28, **30**, 32, 35, 38, 39, 42, 43, 44, 45, 50, 55, 57

Renoir, **4**, 5, 6, 8, 10, 14, 16, 18, 20, 23, **24**, 25, 27, 31, 32, 33, **39**, 45, 46, **47**, 48, **49**, 52, 54, 55, 59

Salon, 7, 12, 13, 14, 19, 21, 25, 28, 38, 39, 42

Sisley, 5, 11, 16, 18, 27, 32, 35, 39, 41, 43, 45, 50, 55, **57**

war, 27, 33

Pages where you can see paintings by the artists are shown in **bold**.

Acknowledgements

Cover: See credits for pages 37, 39, 41, 61. **Title page:** *Self Portrait* by Monet, Private Collection/Photo © Lefevre Fine Art Ltd., London/Bridgeman Art Library. **Page 4:** See credit for page 47. **Page 7:** *Charles X Giving Prizes to Artists at the 1824 Salon* by Heim © RMN/Gérard Blot. **Page 15:** *Déjeuner sur l'Herbe* by Manet © Gallery Collection/Corbis. **Page 22:** *Women in a Garden* by Monet © London Art Archive/Alamy. **Page 24:** *La Grenouillère* by Renoir © Nationalmuseum, Stockholm, Sweden/Bridgeman Art Library. **Page 26:** *Beach at Trouville* by Monet © Trustees of the National Gallery, London. **Page 30:** *Fox Hill* by Pissarro © Trustees of the National Gallery, London. **Page 33:** *Great Wave* by Hokusai, Musée Claude Monet, Giverny, France/Giraudon/Bridgeman Art Library. **Page 34:** *Wild Poppies* by Monet © Gallery Collection/Corbis. **Page 36:** *Cradle* by Morisot © Gallery Collection/Corbis. **Page 37:** *Dancing Class* by Degas, Musée d'Orsay, Paris, France/Bridgeman Art Library. **Page 39:** *Box at the Theatre* by Renoir © Samuel Courtauld Trust, Courtauld Institute of Art Gallery/Bridgeman Art Library. **Page 41:** *Impression: Sunrise* by Monet, Musée Marmottan, Paris, France/Giraudon/Bridgeman Art Library. **Page 47:** *Ball at the Moulin de la Galette* by Renoir, Musée d'Orsay, Paris, France/Giraudon/Bridgeman Art Library. **Page 49:** *Lunch of the Boating Party* by Renoir © Francis G. Mayer/CORBIS. **Page 52:** *Gare St Lazare* by Monet © Trustees of the National Gallery, London. **Page 57:** *Banks of the River Loing* by Sisley © Philadelphia Museum of Art/CORBIS. **Page 61:** *Water Lily Pond* by Monet © Trustees of the National Gallery, London.